The Illusiveness of Gray

The Illusiveness of Gray

Poems by

Carol Smallwood

© 2021 Carol Smallwood. All rights reserved.
This material may not be reproduced in any form, published,
reprinted, recorded, performed, broadcast,
rewritten or redistributed without
the explicit permission of Carol Smallwood.
All such actions are strictly prohibited by law.

Cover design by Shay Culligan

ISBN: 978-1-954353-36-7

Kelsay Books
502 South 1040 East, A-119
American Fork, Utah, 84003

Dedicated to my Grandfather, Charles Drust,
and Aunt, Carolyn Drust Andrews

Foreword

The Infinite Layers of Gray

Empty space, 99.9999%, that's the composition of what we are. And like a spiritual expedition into that space, Carol Smallwood's poetry goes towards the locus of mystery. What appears before us might be a television screen, an empty road, a piece of paper. You can't rest on any one reality. The negative space, the "wonderland," that's where the poet goes. And whether the "illusions" we live with define our lives or not, the mind in these poems continues to explore.

Indeed, there's something almost Escher-like in the way Smallwood's poems present the world, close-ups with doubles, hair reflected in a lightbulb becoming "branches against the moon." And onward we travel, the world transforming, the solid evidence before our eyes shifting restlessly on close inspection, one image blurring into another under concentrated attention with more and more revealed as we go. Worlds within worlds, but also the familiar things of life: vines engulfing a favorite pine, a dragonfly, a grandfather clock, a line in the post office; make no mistake, Smallwood's poems occupy the world as much as they penetrate that world to reveal what lies beneath, the mystery on the other side of seeing.

Smallwood's attention to music is a fundamental part of experiencing these poems as well. Masterful, subtle rhymes and elegant unfurling free verse alternate with patterns and sound constructions of such refined design that they slip by at times almost unnoticed, but the pleasure of returning to these poems is to look into *and* listen while inhabiting these precise creations and know that the reader's journey into the poems is a mirror of the poet's journey into the spaces the poems open up. And this recursive layering of poet and reader, opening inward and outward at the same time, is such a luscious dance of word and thought, as though we were looking through a microscope and seeing world within world until the image resolves in a gaze looking back at us. What a thing!

The center may not hold, Smallwood announces with her preface as she launches from Yeats' decree, but the result is not destruction, the loss is not a thing to despair but a liberty of seeing, of seeing beyond seeing, as when she tells us about the light in the mirror, the image there that once was. Everything is changing, traveling, moving in these poems. And reading them is to be more aware of our place in time as something constantly unfolding. The degrees, the layers, the revealing of something that the moment it appears begins to change again, that is the essence of these poems. What's outside becomes inside because the poet gazes hard enough, and in that beholding, the poet and the "wonder" are one.

All in all, what Smallwood brings us is a marvelous collage of days and thoughts, presented from a floating, critical perspective. The poet is witness, guide, adventurer contemplating what she beholds through the lens of Galileo, Einstein, psychology and myth. What we find here in Smallwood's lovely book is exactly what we would hope to find from a poet in full control of her powers and turning those mechanisms on to everything she sees and knows: truly, a life contemplated.

—Douglas Cole, Poet; Author of *The Blue Island, The Gold Tooth in the Crooked Smile of God,* and several others

Preface

The Earth's no longer the center the Sun, planets, revolve—but we still say the Sun rises in the morning. Faced with so much change in an expanding universe on a galaxy we now know is only one among billions, we may recall William Butler Yeats: "Things fall apart; the centre cannot hold" even if he was writing about society after World War I. The feeling of demotion is increased with the mind-bending knowledge humans are overwhelmingly composed of empty space.

It's a moment during a childhood walk which continues to instill a sense of wonder that was the impetus for *The Illusiveness of Gray*; formal poetry was used when it was a better fit than free verse. There are around 70 poems in the collection, and here's some examples of the formal:

Cinquain: "A Pink Cinquain:
Pantoum: "The Line"
Rondeau: "There Comes Such Days"
Sestina, sans meter: "As American as the Reader's Digest"
Sonnet, sans meter: "Two-Faced Janus"
Tercet: "Constellation Tercets"
Triolet: "Hard to Explain"
Villanelle: "The Color Gray"

Sincere thanks to the foreword writer, the poet, Douglas Cole.

The blurb writers:

Steve Glines, Editor, *Wilderness House Literary Review*;
Robert Erlandson, Ph.D., Professor Emeritus Engineering, Wayne State University; Author, *AWE*, 2019;
Theresa Rodriguez, *Longer Thoughts* (Shanti Arts, 2020);
Evan Mantyk, President, The Society of Classical Poets, Mount Hope, New York;

Maggie Frisch, Editor, *Working Writer*;
C.B. Anderson, Author, *Mortal Soup and the Blue Yonder* and *Roots in the Sky, Boots on the Ground*;
Catherine Keller, Author, *Sonder: A Collection of Poems*.

It is hoped the reader enjoys the poems as much as I did while writing them with the idea behind them expressed so well by J.A. Baker: "The hardest thing of all to see is what is really there."

—Carol Smallwood

Acknowledgments

A Matter of Selection: "A Matter of Lines," "Shopping at Tom's"

Chronicles in Passing: "The Iliad," "A Moment Like No Other"

Compartments: Poems on Nature, Femininity and Other Realms: "Shopping at Tom's"

Divining the Prime Meridian: "Geography," "January Thaw," "Toward Galaxies"

Earth's Daughters: "The House Wrapped Around"

In Hubble's Shadow: "Yesterday a Dragonfly"

In the Measuring: "The Line"

Parentheses Journal: "On the Way"

Patterns: Moments in Time: "Shades of Limbo," "Through the Fog"

Prisms, Particles, and Refractions: "Some Days," "Today the Car," "Trailing Wisps"

Spectrum, University of California, Santa Barbara's College of Creative Studies: "T-Shirts at Wendy's"

The Society of Classical Poets: "Hard to Explain," "A Pink Cinquain"

Water, Earth, Air, Fire, and Picket Fences: "It Was Morning," "A Matter of Lines," "Trailing Wisps"

Whimperbang: "Windy Days"

Contents

Prologue

It Was Morning   19

Part I

The Color Gray	23
Through the Fog	24
Observations from a Car	25
A Moment Like No Other	26
During Covid-19	27
Science Extolls	29
Trailing Wisps	30
January Thaw	31
Mixing Notes	32
A Fast Food Pepsi	33
Some Days	34
Shades of Limbo	35
Vines Graceful Green	36
Master of Nature	37
Triplet of Triolets	38
The Straight	40
On the Way	41
Yesterday a Dragonfly	42
Today There Were	43
Opening a Jar	44
A Prufrock Measurement	45
Chemical Reactions	46
Father of History	47

Part II

The Theory of Time	51
An Ancient Greek	52
A Pink Cinquain	53
A Perspective Triplet	54
While Driving	55
The House Wrapped Around	56
Rural Mailboxes	58
Shopping at Tom's	59
Safety of Predictability	61
Today the Car	62
Every Summer	63
A Matter of Lines	64
Windy Days	65
Mother Goose Questions	66
The Iliad	67
Seeing the Sky	68
Things to Depend On	69
Your Censor	70
Fading Light	71
We Hear	73
An Opera	74
That's My First Wife	75

Part III

Art in Parochial Grade School	79
Hard to Explain	80
T-Shirts at Wendy's	81
Things to Ponder in Waiting Rooms	82
As American as the *Reader's Digest*	83
Reflections	85

Constellation Tercets	86
Toward Galaxies	87
The Line	88
A Facade of Fog	89
Two-Faced Janus	90
The Stamps Had	91
Ads Seniors Rather Not See	92
The Balance Scale	93
Knowing	94
Undeniables by Late Thursday	95
Entanglement	96
Clocks	97
There Comes Such Days	98
Black and White to Color	99
A Remodeling	100
Geography	101
Holding On	102

Epilogue

Fog Hints	105

Prologue

Prologue

It Was Morning

when a sound encouraged
a pause in a childhood walk—

there was movement in fog,
a slipping into trees and mist.

Breathless, I waited shrouded
in white but nothing
could be seen or heard.

It wasn't until years later
I knew the wonder had
become a part of me.

Part I

The Color Gray

The shades are many—plain to subtle: charcoal, pearl, dove
and may describe the politically correct on gender and race
such as: them/their; diversity/multicultural fitting like a glove.

The terms popular with lawyers are ubiquitous and shove
away what occurs as inconclusive, circumstantial with grace:
the shades are many—plain to subtle: charcoal, pearl, dove.

Shades are made combining black and white like the above
making the wide palette we use every day from place to place
including: them/their; diversity/multicultural fitting like a glove.

It takes a discrimination, a willing eye, an artist vision sort of
to appreciate nuances in the variety making our airspace;
the shades are many—plain to subtle: charcoal, pearl, dove.

Sometimes it comes (after a while) that tolerance's a labor of love
when gray creeps into our hair making a soft frame for our face
including: them/their; diversity/multicultural fitting like a glove.

If lucky, tolerance is ours when young and difficult disposing of
prejudice isn't necessary, and our days go by without a trace:
the shades are many—plain to subtle: charcoal, pearl, dove
including: them/their; diversity/multicultural fitting like a glove.

Through the Fog

I knew I was almost home when the marker commemorating Nicolet is glimpsed through fog. Had he this uncertainty, this fear of falling over the edge when he stopped so near what he believed the Northwest Passage?

Odysseus, protected by the gods, returned to faithful Penelope after years being a hero: his passage a success through Scylla and Charybdis.

When I arrived, the unmistakable Lake Nipissing air greeted me, a bird descended in the mist, Icarus falling with melted wings; utility lines drooped as if stretched too often in high-wire acts.

The lake was a layered haze with loud snaps of melting ice, foghorn and sea gulls clearer than I'd remembered: there were no siren songs.

Gusts of blowing ashes from a neighbor's drive encouraged being part body and part ghost. Tree limbs snapped from ice like gunshots while chimney smoke rose sideways stayed by some force.

Observations from a Car

One

Squares were dancing oddly on the road
ahead like a television screen image melting—
it must be pieces of paper.

Approaching slowly with apprehension there
wasn't any paper and the road was the same,
then recalled hologram universes—and wasn't
I composed of 99.9999% empty space?

Two

The post office has four large glass doors
(two in, two out) and a lobby of duplicates—
my car was reflected in two outer ones
as I sat in the parking lot. I waved my
white notepad twice and saw it reflected
to make sure it was my car.

When a customer entered, one reflection
disappeared and then the double reflection
returned when the door shut leaving me
with the theory of parallel universes
and Alice in a place called Wonderland.

A Moment Like No Other

      One day in reading class with See Spot Run words came the word, "Suddenly"; it was in a room with a Sisters of Mercy nun who said if we talked the wood floorboards would separate and we'd fall into Hell.

      Seeing the word, pronouncing Suddenly as if tasting endless possibilities in adult words was a moment like no other—and knew something had changed: being confined had vanished I was invincible.

      Years later viewing Carl Sagan's revised *Cosmos* when an imprisoned Bruno (soon to be burned for heresy) mentally escapes into the infinity of space which he believes, this invincibility became clear.

During Covid-19

I watch store customers through glass twice as I sit in my car
one should only grocery shop every 2 weeks and had my time:
it's the only store on main street with cars—my own bazaar
and needed to see something outside the house at lunchtime.

One should only grocery shop every 2 weeks and had my time:
watching people shop in shadows has been entertaining so far
and needed to see something outside the house at lunchtime:
staying inside every day would be losing my North Star.

Watching people shop in shadows has been entertaining so far
I don't even have to spend, just admire the lighted Pepsi sign.
Staying inside every day would be losing my North Star
it'd felt like I'd been inside forever—well, at least a longtime.

I don't even have to spend, just admire the lighted Pepsi sign
while keeping myself and others virus free—the raised bar.
it'd felt like I'd been inside forever—well, at least a longtime:
one could study a man in his pickup truck smoking a cigar

while keeping myself and others virus free—the raised bar
social distancing and wearing masks the new design—
one could study a man in his pickup truck smoking a cigar:
week after week one had to accept it as being normal, fine.

Social distancing and wearing masks the new design—
the large plate glass has become Plato's cave, then a bell jar:
week after week one had to accept it as being normal, fine,
and couldn't tell what was inside or out the window afar:

the large plate glass has become Plato's cave, then a bell jar:
it's the only store on main street with cars—my own bazaar
and couldn't tell what was inside or out the window afar;
I watch store customers through glass twice as I sit in my car.

Science Extolls

a star or leaf through equations, graphs,
telescope/microscope probes, journal
studies, Nobel theories—truly stunning
finds: still it's equally astonishing that
just 4% of the universe is known.

Yet seeing nature with scientific eyes
drains wonder and I return to Arachne's
new woven spider webs, Apollo rising
in the sun, hearing Mark Twain:
"Don't part with your illusions.
When they are gone you may still
exist but you have ceased to live."

Trailing Wisps

Hearing a distant
Train and picturing
Trailing wisps of white,
I realized with
Surprise that trains
Hadn't smoked for
Years; that
Conjured grace of
Trailing wisps had
Been illusions—and
Smoke wouldn't
Been white.

The whistle
Became reedy
Disjointed threads
The closer the train
Came. When it left
Quavering, as if
Entangled in the wind,
I turned into a wisp
Of white and trailed
It out of town.

January Thaw

Snow fog confirms
belief in another dimension
invisible as black matter as
eyes strain for the familiar.

With air so fresh it's best
not to inhale too deep too long,
or remember memories of spring—
January thaw being brief.

Mixing Notes

Have you ever considered perfume to be combined scents in all likelihood? Their Latin name, per fumus (through smoke) is quite appropriate, relevant: jasmine, rose, patchouli, muguet, ylang-ylang, vanilla, mimosa, sandalwood.

Perfume, used for thousands of years—using it changes through adulthood claiming it a gift of romance not just on Valentine's Day have you ever considered perfume to be combined scents in all likelihood?

The making of perfume is described by Pliny the Elder which has stood many readings—its manufacture having undergone steady development: jasmine, rose, patchouli, muguet, ylang-ylang, vanilla, mimosa, sandalwood.

Other familiar notes are: orchid, passionflower, honeysuckle, magnolia wood and it's often difficult to detect which scents are the most preeminent: have you ever considered perfume to be combined scent in all likelihood?

The first recorded chemist, a Babylonian woman, used solvents which did much groundbreaking, an improvement we can't underestimate; jasmine, rose, patchouli, muguet, ylang-ylang, vanilla, mimosa, sandalwood.

So become acquainted with what particular notes which you would reflect you, become your signature—an important part of beguilement. Have you ever considered perfume to be combined scent in all likelihood? Jasmine, rose, patchouli, muguet, ylang-ylang, vanilla, mimosa, sandalwood.

A Fast Food Pepsi

to the right caught my eye—bubbles were popping
so I moved the glass, lining my eyes with the
reflection of the lamp overhead: shutting one eye
made the clear reflection move.

Bending closer showed strands of my hair against
the bulb like branches against the Moon; a halo
formed inside the rim of the carbonated drink
which swirled, bubbles disappearing at random.

Two glasses appeared when looking: a gray
colored lamp at the angle of an orbiting satellite
and a larger upright yellow shade with bulb—
but how could that happen?

When the yellow bulb grew top and bottom peaks
a chill came not unlike being with Columbus
afraid of falling off the Earth and stopped looking
after wondering about the 4th dimension—
and what would people think of ogling a glass?

Some Days

In the spring when pushing a cart down aisles she
wore a tiara of seed pearls and in the fall, rubies.
Some days trains were of ermine, other days crackling
taffeta; her diamonds the size of robin eggs on both
hands and the size of lima beans as buttons; samples
extended in paper cups were not Wisconsin cider
but French champagne in long stem crystal handed
out not by gum chewing Babs or Trudi in uniforms
with slips showing, but ladies in flowing velvet.
She imagined what they (her subjects) were saying
about her beauty and clothes, how they'd die for her.
Tears filled her eyes seeing her funeral procession
with grief-stricken subjects tossing rose petals.

Shades of Limbo

The vertical line of spindles on the familiar bed headboard
were becoming visible—confirming a night without sleep.

Light slipped through closed blinds: the room getting form
where the ceiling ended and the wall began evident by
different shades of gray—the ghostly chair by the window
acquiring shape.

Perhaps it would be good to get up, end this limbo but
the lace edging you sewed to a sheet brings stability,
and you're grateful for a pen in your hand but wondered
if the words to describe where the door was would
be readable.

Earplugs make a black/white silent film and rising,
walk like Charlie Chaplin for courage.

Vines Graceful Green

progressed one summer on the
utility line above the road traveled
making one recall ivy of old estates;
the plush vines climbed the utility
pole from greenery below.

Then one of my pines looked as if
struck by the Siberian meteor,
and when cut still stood bound
by sinuous vines with red
berries that drained its life.

Distrustful am I of beloved
bittersweet now—its foreign
invasive variety bringing
a garden of evil traveling
under ground and tree tops.

Master of Nature

It is that something in the soul which says, Rage on, Whirl on, I tread master here and everywhere—Master of the spasms of the sky and of the shatter of the sea, Master of nature and passion and death, and of all terror and all pain.
—Walt Whitman

I wonder what Whitman would've thought when thirty-four years after his death, Hubble found the Milky Way to be only one of billions of galaxies and three years later the universe was expanding?

There is something we also can't help thinking—climate warming; and about being master of "all terror and all pain."

Triplet of Triolets

Unsettling Wonder

When standing still in a parking lot and the car beside you moves
there's a terrible sinking feeling you're the one moving instead
bringing wonder about multiple universes—doubts hard to remove
when standing still in a parking lot and the car beside you moves.
Should theoretical physicist Greene's nine multiverses be approved?
Is cosmologist Tegmark right in his four universe levels, or mislead?
When standing still in a parking lot and the car beside you moves,
there's a terrible sinking feeling you're the one moving instead.

To Lessen Quilting Tangles

Use thread coated with starches, waxes, a finishing additive glaze,
cut not too long with a small needle for small stitches close
    together.
A glacé finish makes for fewer knots and less frustrating sewing
    days.
Use thread coated with starches, waxes, a finishing additive glaze
to reduce pesky entanglements in sewing quilts during any phase
for less abrasion when pulling thread through cut pieces altogether.
Use thread coated with starches, waxes, a finishing additive glaze,
cut not too long with a small needle for small stitches close
    together.

Camelot

Did King Arthur of Camelot and his Knights of the Round Table
ever live? Legends are many—a popular figure of romance.
John F. Kennedy's early presidency was compared to Camelot
    fable:
did King Arthur of Camelot and his Knights of the Round Table
ever appear in reliable history? He isn't found in any that's stable
but lives in poems, tales, legends, and modern song and dance.
Did King Arthur of Camelot and his Knights of the Round Table
ever live? Legends are many—a popular figure of romance.

The Straight

There's not much that's straight in the natural state: much is round, curved. It could be opposite of course since around only 4% is what we can see—dark energy and dark matter making up the rest.

Science says the hexagon cones are the best possible shape: the most economical for storing honey, even better than squares or rectangles.

After driving, I've concluded roads try to be straight but seldom are—even my driveway isn't; the painted lines on crosswalks makes one dizzy: but it's better that way as it helps prevent dozing.

On the Way

from town today there was a square large field, all white
dazzling under a late summer sky with Queen Anne's Lace:
near Gary's Funeral Home, lace flooded the field with light—
the celebration of such delicate abandon seemed out of place.

Dazzling under a late summer sky with Queen Anne's Lace
after the new addition to the County Commission on Aging
the celebration of such delicate abandon seemed out of place:
under lofty rolling cumulus August clouds a brash staging.

After the new addition to the County Commission on Aging
edged by a rim, a gray cemetery of felled trees by the woods,
under lofty rolling cumulus August clouds a brash staging:
an unexpected stranger on the outskirts of the neighborhood.

Edged by a rim, a gray cemetery of felled trees by the woods
near Gary's Funeral Home lace flooded the field with light—
an unexpected stranger on the outskirts of the neighborhood:
from town today there was a square large field, all white.

Yesterday a Dragonfly

caught my eye when I was
hanging clothes to dry

Resting transparent wings
it moved its head as if
studying me

When I returned with pen
and paper it'd vanished
like yesterday's dream

It came today and flexed
six legs—till I fetched
a magnifying glass

Today There Were

whopping 50# bags of 2 kinds of flour, yellow popcorn, 4 kinds of
    rice
for sale with gallon size olive oil, 30# pails of mayonnaise, tartar
sauce—Gulliver Brobdingnag size bottles of ginger, pepper,
cinnamon, allspice.

whopping 50# bags of 2 kinds of flour, yellow popcorn, 4 kinds of
rice described in English, French, and Spanish, encouraged a
    survey
thrice along with a good calculation of the muscles of each
    shelfing worker:

whopping 50# bags of 2 kinds of flour, yellow popcorn, 4 kinds of
rice on sale with gallon size olive oil, 30# pails of mayonnaise,
    tartar sauce.

Opening a Jar

bringing my whopping jar of olives to the checkout, I asked it be
opened as the last one had to be returned, opened with special
    gloves

in the back room after my handyman had tried his best. The
checkout tried—the husky assistant at the counter tried—the
    manager twisted till his face turned red.

About to suggest trying another jar, a passing customer
said she opened jars at home by pushing a screwdriver under the
    lid.

Recalling all of my handyman's efforts with tools, I doubted the
suggestion; the husky assistant got a screw driver and it worked—
the vacuum, invisible, escaped.

A Prufrock Measurement

I'm a connoisseur—how long drinks keep cold
and how much they may drip down sides:
an expert of how much ice they'll hold.
Wendy's red, white, gold, cups abide
with the redheaded girl taking one in stride.

McDonald's cups have the word thirst,
and a running Ronald tossing cups in trash.
I'm not sure where golden arches appeared first
but they've surely multiplied, dispersed
widely around the world without much abash.

Subway's cups have arrows on the first and last
letters of Subway; images of ice one presumes
is to carry one far away from despairing places
where women talk of Michelangelo with bored faces
and other topics one dares not to assume.

Chemical Reactions

The Sun's a nuclear reactor—no longer
Helios riding a golden chariot: will beauty,
wonder be accepted as chemical reactions
by burgeoning neuroscience?

Wordsworth noted: "Sweet is the lore that
Nature brings; Our meddling intellect/
Misshapes the beauteous forms of things:
We murder to dissect."

I can understand spears evolving for
human survival but surely compassion's
an ingredient in quality civilization—
or is that too a chemical reaction?

Gazing at the night sky was calming,
full of wonder as a child but knowing
now why stars glow and twinkle and
so much more—I long for the mystery.

Father of History

Herodotus is chronicled as the first to arrange history a systematic way
and yet what he compiled is in quite an entertaining format and style
that also borrowed on traditional story-telling and myths it is safe to say.

Born in the Persian Empire, his name is still highly regarded, a mainstay
in the study of history—*The Histories,* regarded as written without guile:
Herodotus is chronicled as the first to arrange history a systematic way.

His writing on the Greco-Persian Wars, the long collision of which may
be read as accounts in the clash between East and West enmity or bile
 that also borrowed on traditional story-telling and myths it is safe to say.

The Roman, Cicero, called him, "The Father of History," in his day
which has remained despite much investigation, discussion, and trial:
Herodotus is chronicled as the first to arrange history a systematic way.

His writing explores lives of famous men, and battles holding much sway
such as Marathon, Thermopylae, with geographical digressions in mile

that also borrowed on traditional story-telling and myths it is
　　safe to say.
Historians praise his historiographic narrative in classes to this day encouraging some specialists to question his work, continue to rile: Herodotus is chronicled as the first to arrange history a systematic
　　way
　　　　that also borrowed on traditional story-telling and myths it is
　　　　safe to say.

Part II

The Theory of Time

It's been over a century since Einstein's theory of relativity—one which I don't understand except the part that time isn't absolute, recalling the summer before entering high school was equal to all the years since 2000. The summer was a time of waiting, wondering about high school while cutting out pictures, cartoons from the neighbor's *Saturday Evening Post* and arranging them in scrapbooks; worrying how unprepared I was. The years after 2000 were getting used to starting the year 20 instead of 19—grasping to capture, understand, adapt a changing theory of time.

An Ancient Greek

It's become an icon: the blindfolded woman holding a scale set
in one hand and a sword in the other—accepted symbols of law:
the robed Themis was known for clear vision so we're in her debt.
It's become an icon: the blindfolded woman holding a scale set,
the sword is sheathed, her poised hand on the hilt quite correct.
Themis wasn't blindfolded till Christian times—luck of the draw
it's become an icon: the blindfolded woman holding a scale set
in one hand and a sword in the other—accepted symbols of law.

A Pink Cinquain

Pink has become a favored cultural color, more subtle, less primitive than red: black mixed with pink is considered seductive, innocent when used with white and acquired its own name just in the late 17th century it's commonly read. In the 1940s, blue for boys, pink for girls became the custom, an accepted rite; Mamie Eisenhower's 1953 inaugural pink gown was a major fashion
   highlight

and Jacqueline Kennedy helped to make it associated with high-fashion spread although the famous portrait, "Pinkie" symbolized youth in simple daylight. There are amazing hues of pink in rose, dahlia, hyacinth, and others flower beds varying from light to deepest pink attracting insects—pollination widespread. Names for pink—cotton candy, cherry blossom pink, and fuchsia give delight;

tickled pink, seeing pink elephants, in the pink, are sayings that have spread. Breast Cancer Awareness uses pink ribbons to stand out in the public limelight with distinction to combat a wide health problem. In *Young Goodman Brown,* Faith wears a pink hair ribbon to symbolize innocence; in *Little Women,* bound ribbons appear on Amy's twins. All told—pink packs a lot of cultural
   insight.

A Perspective Triplet

Not a Car

was at the 4-way stoplight and
looked around in hopes of seeing
one, or even better—a cement
mixer in carnival colors.

When the light turned, the rear
view mirror gradually telescoped
the stoplight until all became
little cat feet fog.

Before

we used telescopes, one explanation was the
Sun was Apollo driving a chariot with horses
(they each had their own names) across the sky.

Now we know the Sun's a chemical reaction
and there's many larger—but it's still more
satisfying to see Apollo and his horses.

When a Certain Age

if you're a woman be prepared to be called
young lady, sweetheart, honey, dear, as
terms of endearment; it's best not to recall
those you used for others not long ago.

While Driving

The clouds, layered, remote,
shift like today's truth in more
shades of gray than were able
to grasp even when not driving.

Pine trees skewer the ground—
frilled green toothpicks standing
next to slim bare-limbed maple
like at a neighborhood party.

Day after day, facing roads rural mail
boxes boast their longevity with rust
over upstarts of colored molded plastic—
while others, shoved…bend in surprise.

Frost's poem about choosing the grassy road
not the more traveled in the yellow wood
is seemingly simple, presented as student fare:
for most—words to recall passing exits.

The House Wrapped Around

as if I'd never left, my feet automatically
adapting to the spot that dipped, and
without looking I knew the exact distance
between the windows even without the
television or stereo.

The heavy doors did provide a feeling
of solidity until one stuck—and the panic
only calmed by the window above the
kitchen sink where I'd studied clouds.

Despite the happiness being with the kids,
I remembered: "How do you know I'm mad?"
said Alice. "You must be," said the
Cheshire Cat," or you wouldn't have come
here."

Brylcreem, cigarettes, and antiseptic clung to
the bedroom once shared with Cal; only two
mirrors remained arranged so they endlessly
repeated me till I disappeared.

There'd been a mirror the night before I
married that'd given wavy reflections
while packing away girlhood diaries.

Now the stripes in the yellow wallpaper
mocked, "So you thought you'd get away?
Cal said you never would."

The yellow wallpaper became that in the
story about a wife who peels it to free
the woman she thinks trapped.
Her husband called her, little girl—
so did mine.

Rural Mailboxes

My favorite? An imposing homemade mound of
local stones and mortar with only the mailbox
door visible—homage to pyramid longevity.

Shopping at Tom's

Tears filled her eyes imagining her funeral
procession extending to the dairy counter.
Aisle 4 featured stacked boxes of fortune cookies—
removing just one bottom box would bring them
crashing; she smiled as she ducked under
a banner of chickens in yellow straw hats

followed by turkeys in hiking boots. After a
hysterectomy did they package your remains in a
paper sack like the gizzard, heart, liver, neck,
inside a roasting chicken? Chives, cilantro leaves,
cinnamon. It was good to see the Morton Salt girl
under her umbrella still pouring salt. She'd used

saltboxes with the top and bottom removed to hold
gifts for the kids at Christmas. When she was
walking past the peanuts she remembered buying
small gifts. She went to see if the SunMaid girl
in her red bonnet with long ties was still
effortlessly holding that huge tray of green grapes.

She recalled the restaurant next door, listening to
old men talk about how rabbits made runways in the
woods, about walking in circles in the snow. The
steam rose from the coffee maker by the men sitting
closely shoulder to shoulder, saw again the holes
in their shoes, holes that gave them personality.

The men were always the same men on the same stools.
Next time she'd check the labels of Clabber Girl Baking
Powder: the girl carrying the plate of perfectly tall,

uniform, stacked golden brown biscuits was always
there with a Mona Lisa smile—but was she walking
to put them on the table or on the way to eat them?

The sitting woman on the label seemed to be sewing but
could be plucking a goose, it was hard to see clearly.
One of the tabloids read: *Moses Spotted Walking
on Miami Beach.* Had other women felt failures when
their biscuits never matched those on the label,
used a magnifying glass to see the sitting woman.

Safety of Predictability

A lack of sleep encourages awareness
in the safety of predictability:
you think of clocks, the rhythm of day and night—
that total quiet is rare. Sleeplessness
encourages losing civility,
a definite increase in irritability
fearing others know what you're thinking
and will banish you elsewhere.

You think of clocks, the rhythm of day and night—
that total quiet is rare. There's fear
of the unknown, an uneasiness gravity
will come to an end, fearing others know
what you're thinking will banish you elsewhere
and you fight the sinking feeling
it could be the end—useless to pretend.

There's fear of the unknown,
an uneasiness gravity will come to an end;
sleeplessness encourages losing civility,
a definite increase in irritability
and you fight the sinking feeling it
could be the end—useless to pretend.
A lack of sleep encourages
awareness in the safety of predictability.

Today the Car

ahead had a sticker: As Real as It Gets. It was windy—
bags and flyers scurrying the street.

When I got in the lab room, the chair had the same hospital
auxiliary bluebird pillow, employees the same photo badge
stars and stripes. The aide abandoned my arm for my hand
and didn't respond to my question, "How much you need?"
so watched the wall clock and wondered why magazines
featured makeup to make you look natural.

The car wash had a grinning boy with muffled ears who
emerged in the mist waving white towels in a jet roar.
After reaching *Put Car in Drive When You See This Sign*
I followed the tracks of those before.

Driving home, the tips of corn emerging in spring in such
straight lines had become cracking gold—in July their
uniforms sinuous emerald.

Every Summer

mayflies (also called dayflies) swarm the
streetlight for a few nights: the closer
to the light the more frantically they fly.

In the morning, those that didn't fly away
flutter on the road drawing birds; cars soon
erase traces.

Their order, named after the mythical
Ephemerides is an allusion to their brief life
although fossils go back millions of years.

Females deposit eggs on water then die;
the males deposit sperm like crop dusters.

I released one in a spider's web, but didn't
stay to see if it could fly away.

A Matter of Lines

1

It's a toss-up which postal
clerk you get: the one always
smiling or the frowning one
you think more sincere

Both have the tone of
priests in confessionals
murmuring, "What's inside?"

When finished, you pretend not
to see the others waiting,
departing with downcast eyes

2

Corn the color of worn
gold in straight lines
molded by prevailing wind,
graceful before the fall

3

Line upon line spun off
easily in dreams:
on waking they
turned into balls—
bouncing off reason
they tangled

Windy Days

I often walked the beach on windy days because the waves
carried me where I'd never been and erased footprints.

The waves held secrets I kept trying to snatch but always
failed no matter how often they kept repeating themselves,
no two the same. Sometimes I'd bring a book but reading
seemed disrespectful.

I tried to imagine Nicolet's wonder seeing Lake Michigan
looking for the Orient. What'd happened to the Chinese
damask robe Nicolet had worn greeting the Winnebago's
at Green Bay? A gust of wind overturned his canoe—
he must've known how thin the layer of birch was so why
hadn't he learned to swim? Why hadn't anyone saved him?
But perhaps he'd been alone. After countless uncharted
rivers and lakes, drowning at familiar Sillery must've been
a surprise.

The gray sky looked restful—and I looked for a long
but all that changed were undulating clouds like a child
practicing the letter "M" until a flock of birds crisscrossed
them out.

Mother Goose Questions

One, two, buckle my shoe, three, four, shut the door;
Cock a doodle do! My dame has lost her shoe;
Old Mrs. Hubbard's cupboard deserves a low score—
did the cow who jumped over the moon give a moo?

Cock a doodle do! My dame has lost her shoe;
as years go I recall traditional Mother Goose more:
did the cow who jumped over the moon give a moo,
do you think Bobby Shafto returned safely to shore?

As years go I recall old Mother Goose more:
rhymes are ageless, each generation are brand-new.
Do you think Bobby Shafto returned safely to shore?
Did the kittens who lost their mittens give any clue?

Rhymes are ageless, each generation are brand-new.
Did the old lady in a shoe have so many children—a slew?
Did the kittens who lost their mittens give any clue?
Do you think the boy blowing his horn only wore blue?

Did the old lady in a shoe have so many children—a slew?
Old Mrs. Hubbard's cupboard deserves a low score.
Do you think the boy blowing his horn only wore blue?
One, two, buckle my shoe, three, four, shut the door.

The Iliad

The Iliad, considered the earliest work in the Western literary tradition is one of the most famous and loved chronicles recounting events in the Trojan War, and Siege of Troy—chronicles used in later renditions.

Although usually attributed to Homer, *The Iliad* is an older addition an inheritance of singer-poets—it's uncertain Homer ever lived, had kin: *The Iliad* is considered the earliest work in Western literary tradition.

The poem's lines are dactylic hexameter, a formal rhythm audition making it easier to memorize, some phrases are repeatedly akin… the Trojan War, Siege of Troy—chronicles for other later renditions.

The theme is one of war and peace: a mix of horror, glory: submission both of heroism and viciousness questioning the heavy cost of a win—*The Iliad,* considered the earliest work in the Western literary tradition.

The many gods and goddesses mock or copy the human condition are used as allegories, psychological purposes, for comedy built-in: the Trojan War and Siege of Troy—chronicles used in later renditions.

Poems were recited at festivals and for those in important position by singers beating the measure with staffs maybe covered by skin. *The Iliad,* considered the earliest work in the Western literary tradition: the Trojan War, and Siege of Troy—chronicles used in later renditions.

Seeing the Sky

What would it have been like for Galileo—
the first to see the sky closer than anyone else?
What absolute wonder he must've felt—and
immense loneliness.

The magnification of the telescope he perfected
(30 times what could be seen before) was enough
to have the Catholic Church put him on trial for
heresy.

Van Gogh is credited to have been the first to
paint the sky as a main subject with *Starry Night*
a depiction that couldn't have been more different
than Galileo's realism.

Things to Depend On

1
Watching "What's My Line?" with guests like Eleanor
Roosevelt: women (called Miss or Mrs.) in white glove
and dresses, men in suits, ties—cigarettes and furs.

2
There's a town I drive through where people walk streets
and not sidewalks; no matter if it's spring, summer, fall,
or winter they walk singly, in pairs or groups no matter
the time of day: men, women, children. They never give a glance
or move out of the way: granted they don't walk directly in the
driver's path, just near enough to make it is the driver's job to
navigate around them—accommodation expected. The wide
sidewalks are in good shape, plowed in winter. And I keep
asking: why?

3
No matter the season mud puddles come and go—
rain, melted snow in depressions shallow or deep
reflecting with dependable clarity making one dizzy.
I approach the edges with fear recalling school tales of hell
opening up.

Your Censor

Memory believes before knowing remembers.
—William Faulkner

During the day, dreams flit like humming bird wings—part of you wants to remember, another doesn't. You're grateful that your subconscious blocks dreams it judges too much to handle.

Fading Light

The framed family tree on the living room wall was getting a vagueness which meant light was retreating as it hung opposite the picture window. On cloudy days there wasn't much difference in dawn and sunset as blinds defuse the direction of the sun. Alone as if the Cheshire Cat waiting to disappear in the light.

I distrusted coming night: my ancestors valued light and thought it fitting that we now know most of the universe is unknown black energy and black matter. Things go bump in the night not just on Halloween; checking under beds and behind doors is ongoing with an ever-active labyrinth called the subconscious.

A movement revealed something snakelike causing my heart to beat faster—only a ribbon in fading light hanging over a chair. I studied what I could see: the face of the clock, the label on the back massager, around the edges of the window—the rest of the room imperceptibly being washed of any remaining color.

Through the blinds I sensed something but it was probably only a shrub hit by rain beginning to fall— spring had its own unique sound of muffled thunder. I wasn't sure if my writing was clear in the dim light and should see if I could find more paper not knowing how many more words were possible but had to push until it was time to get dinner.

Yesterday had a lot of sun and heard that there's nothing that travels faster than light and until warp drives to travel the curving fabric of spacetime, can we hope to go further than the Moon. It was only in my lifetime we knew of other galaxies besides the Milky Way and that only about 4% of the universe is known. Why didn't I know sooner the tilt of Earth's axis determines the seasons?

Light was no longer coming through the blinds so it was time to turn on lamps—some early people made pictures not using stars but from empty black space.

We Hear

the universe is expanding even faster than was
thought—our concern considerably increased since
learning Earth wasn't the center of what we saw in the
sky and our Milky Way relegated to only one among
billions.

And to know that humans are overwhelmingly made of
of empty space—discovering what lies deep within each
of ourselves more than a lifelong concern.

An Opera

I'll always remember *Aida*: how the woman sitting behind described how suddenly rain fell in Bermuda, the rustle of programs, the excitement in a student's voice about the discovery of a new galaxy—the warmth of Mitchell's shoulder against mine for the first time and basked in being a bird that'd found its way.

There was no mention of when I'd be returning home on the broad balcony where we stood: I was a princess with silver buttons being admired during intermission. But the buried alive scene in the final act made me whisper, "I can't stay. I'll wait outside." He stood with me by the white Doric columns on the steps in the warm

night air until terror faded and panic of suffocation lost its grip. I remembered smiling at the attendant when he asked, "Did you and your wife enjoy the performance" because it meant we looked like we belonged together. The closed red and gold curtain seemed a sunset, a final farewell, and clutched the program of *Aida*,

proof the night was real—and to stop tears, wondered what the woman had looked like who'd described how suddenly rain fell in Bermuda who'd sat behind us wearing Estée Lauder and if she had season tickets and would sit in the same seat in the theater—and if she was happy. When Mitchell walked me to my

car in the darkness, his coat blew against me, a benediction I knew had to be lasting. Would I ever know the new galaxy the student had said with such excitement had just been discovered?

That's My First Wife

Inspired by Robert Browning's, "My Last Duchess"

you see in the painting there by
my coat of arms: did you know
white symbolizes sincerity
in heraldry?

Do you like the new walls?
Oh—so you've read, "The
Yellow Wallpaper."

One of my family tales is vertical
burial for the deserving: trying to
escape only got them in deeper.

I'd entertain her with legends
to help toughen her but near the
end had to take the car keys away.

She became so weak she'd
wouldn't listen and turned
rigid as this knife; the handle has
my monogram but be careful—
the blade's very sharp.

Part III

Art in Parochial Grade School

was using prescribed colors for religious pictures once a week. We learned on a color wheel which colors were analogous and complementary while crayons stayed within black lines.

The most fun was discovering that blue and yellow made green; red and yellow made orange; mixing black and white to make gray held no attraction since lines were already black, paper white like nun habits.

Hard to Explain

After the Holy Grail of physics, the Big Bang,
came the battle of anti-matter and matter
which is hard to explain scientifically or in slang.
The Holy Grail of physics, the Big Bang
shouldn't be considered a fool's harangue
since experts named it after prolonged chatter.
After the Holy Grail of physics, the Big Bang,
came the battle of anti-matter and matter.

T-Shirts at Wendy's

A girl carrying a baby in a sequin tutu t-shirt's read:
"Life is Like Toilet Paper, You're Either On A Roll Or
You're Out"

A laughing boy with LOVE IS A disappearing under
a black t-shirt with flame letters: "See You in Hell"

A woman staring into space in her thirties with a
silent young boy: "I Fear Nothing, I'm a Nurse"

Things to Ponder in Waiting Rooms

Particles passing through you
from the Big Bang

How to explain General Relativity
or Special Relativity to someone
next to you

To a man riding a bicycle, another
next to him isn't moving if both are
going the same speed

99.9% of life forms are extinct

Every breath you take has atoms
of others who've lived

What Hubble must've felt
discovering another solar system

As American as the *Reader's Digest*

I called the Avon Lady to help me feel more at home
and looked forward to a possible way to meet others.
"Do you know you have a wasp's nest by your door?"
"Oh, is that right?" I asked trying to sound concerned.
The Avon lady extended a calendar saying, "I know it's
late for a calendar but aren't the colors so pastel?"

To my nod, she added, "The pictures have such fresh pastel
appeal don't they? You know, I don't have the breeze at home
that you do here," I saw her nose carefully detecting its
scent—my neighbor's dairy herd. She sat not as others,
back not touching the couch figuring me out, concerned
where I fit in the scheme while glaring at my screen door.

"My grandchildren are husky boys that knock on my door
asking for my baked cookies but wish I could buy pastel
dresses for girls." I looked at her catalog concerned
with remembering, bringing back love: "You rush home
to greet him with laughter and love," girls and others
dipping hands in a dappled stream smiling like it's

always spring. I see slim models making me believe it's
the only way women should be, children going out the door
with baskets of strawberries. Rose petals and others
graced pages that matched the lipstick, a pale pastel
called Eternal Blush, worn by the Avon Lady. Her home
I imagined as pale, matching; she was concerned

that I would get the next catalog out, quite concerned
if I wasn't home she'd give the bag an extra twist so it's
sure wind wouldn't carry it off. Avon gives a sense of home,

of belonging as American as the *Reader's Digest.* My door
knob would hang the next catalog. Did filters make the pastel
shades misty vanishing outlines for creams, and others?

Even lotion (pour le corps) had pastel labels, others
too, but saw that catalogs were also now concerned
with cell phones. She confided, "Women like to use pastel
so much. It's so delightful, so feminine, romantic, it's
so flattering, comforting, my dear," going out the door;
I'd hang the calendar she'd extended on a wall in my home.

I'd look forward to the next catalog from the Avon Lady,
will watch my front and side door with a concerned look,
guessing next year's calendar will also be pastel.

Reflections

Growing up I put metal curlers on my fingers to keep them slim,
held my breath for a smaller waist, peered in mirrors to see
magazine ads.

When married, I basked in the glow of my husband's image in
Jackie Kennedy white gloves and when he no longer looked,
turned to tie-dye and madras.

Then I was in a bedroom alone that echoed, a beveled mirror
repeating endlessly till I disappeared in the mirror behind.

When children began dating, I attributed lines to the sun—
a hysterectomy's nothing big—there's time enough for love.

Then gray hair dressed me as in clouds in a Greek play;
I stand now in store aisles to prove I have form, ponder why
car passenger mirrors read: Objects in Mirror Are Closer
than They Appear.

Constellation Tercets

Orion, the mythical Greek hunter with his companion bow
    said to be an easy constellation to spot in night sky
        is mentioned in Virgil, Homer, and the Bible.
That Orion's brightest stars, Rigel and Betelgeuse,
    and the two others said to make them is to defy
        vision and requires much speculation.
But it could be a Rorschach—each of us interprets
    what we view—a long accepted cut and dry
        concept why there's so many constellations.

The constellation, Leo, said to look like a lion that in
    Greek myth had fur that couldn't be pierced, claws
        sharper than any sword.
The outline made of Leo seen in many books looks more
    like a tea kettle or an iron to me—giving pause
        it was a man who named it.
Tradition says the huge lion was killed by Hercules as part
    of his twelve labors which makes sense because
        I've never seen a lion in the sky.

Toward Galaxies

As a child, death's a break
break from school

In college, a mix of
philosophy and biology

When children come, time's
dismissed by actuary tables

Then, a 7% chance of surviving
cancer you live Dickinson's:
"After great pain, a formal
feeling comes."

And the conclusion that
you're not the center of things:
inch by inch the Moon's moving
from Earth and you're stuff of stars

The Line

Today the fast food place line was extra long—
customers waiting like in a church confession
obtaining support by being one of the throng
in line with other fellow souls in procession.

Customers waiting like in a church confession
contemplating photos of shakes, fries, and cones
in line with other fellow souls in procession
rationalizing one day they'll just be bones—

contemplating photos of shakes, fries, and cones,
pushing aside New Year Resolutions not long ago
rationalizing one day they'll just be bones
thinking eating healthy is a tough row to hoe.

Pushing aside New Year Resolutions not long ago
ignoring cholesterol, sugar, starch, and fat
thinking eating healthy is a tough row to hoe
instead believe themselves with stomach flat

ignoring cholesterol, sugar, starch, and fat,
staring at the wall menu with caloric red flags
instead believe themselves with stomach flat
disregarding additions to hip saddle bags.

Staring at the wall menu with caloric red flags
obtaining support by being one of the throng
disregarding additions to hip saddle bags—
today the fast food place line was extra long.

A Facade of Fog

Recently I watched *Columbo,* the Emmy/Golden
Globe winning series. With a rumpled raincoat,
disheveled hair, cigar ashes that scatter, laces that
break—the LAPD detective weaves a disguise.

The first episode in 1971, introduces Columbo's
battered gray coupe that he calls "very rare" when
comments are made. He asks dimes for calls,
litters crime scenes, arrives sneezing with allergies.

His pockets hold hard-boiled eggs to identification;
in one episode his coat conceals pajamas. When he
appears in a new coat (he says his wife got it), he
returns to his old one he says helps him think.

Mrs. Columbo, the Ann Landers column reader
he often mentions is never seen—his comments
reveal as much about him as her and the culture
of the times; their home's kept in fog.

Columbo (his first name's unknown) talks about
aunts, uncles, nieces, nephews we never see. His
cigar swirling smoke and his iconic line: "Just
one more thing" builds illusion.

Two-Faced Janus

The worship of Janus goes back to Romulus even before the start of the city of Rome as the god of beginnings, gates, transitions, time, duality, doorways, passages, and endings. Janus presided over the part of ending of conflict and war and peace—his temple doors open anytime in time of war, were closed to mark the peace. As a god of transitions, he had many temples erected to him and was connected with activities pertaining to birth, journeys and exchanges, and associated with missions with Portunus, a harbor god, concerned with travelling safety agility. It is agreed that the first month of the year, January, is for Janus acclaimed for having two opposite faces, the ability to see all things in past phase and future. Around 450 BCE, January became the first 30 days reclaimed on the Roman calendar; later Julius Caesar added a day to make it 31 days. Janus remains a solid example of the middle ground—between barbarity and civilization, youth and adulthood, urban cities and insularity.

The Stamps Had

PTSD in big letters, **healing** in smaller letters on rusty black—stark with a few green leaves. How many knew it stood for Posttraumatic Stress Disorder row after row on a sheet? It was now formally recognized by the American Medical Association. Maybe using one stamp at a time wouldn't overwhelm—we would become aware?

Ads Seniors Rather Not See

Tracker for Miles Walked Daily
Life Expectancy Actuaries
Technology for Dummies
Weight Reduction Pills
Lawyers Specializing in Wills
Over 40 Online Dating
Prunes Shipped Regularly
Swimwear for the Mature

The Balance Scale

An ancient Egyptian funerary guide shows the balance scale,
a heart placed on one scale, a feather balancing the other side:
the *Book of the Dead* illustrates a commonly used scale in its tale.
An ancient Egyptian funerary book shows the balance scale
depicting what early Egyptians believed after death in great detail
and provides information of scales in ancient history—a real guide.
a heart placed on one scale, a feather balancing the other side.

Knowing

We can just reach (a tantalizing almost) to when the
Big Bang happened—will it become accepted that life's
a matter of chemistry, love a behavioral adaptation, beauty
symmetry of the perceiver, our intelligence surpassed by
pixels on a screen? Understanding our subconscious is still
a frontier as is what lies underground beneath our feet.

Copernicus, who advanced the theory the earth wasn't the
the center of the universe—wisely didn't present this heresy
heresy until on his deathbed. Rutherford was afraid to step
on the floor the morning after discovering atoms are mostly
empty space—and who could blame him?

Undeniables by Late Thursday

*

One has to admire dandelions—the crack
and cranny entrepreneurs using parachute
seed distribution.

*

When I asked a male novelist: "Was it difficult
making a woman your main character?"
he replied, "Men and women I consider are
really much the same." Was it true or was he
only young?

*

Humpty Dumpty's Lawyer Claims Wall Was Faulty
Wee Winnie Winkle Under House Arrest
Jack Sprat And Wife On Oprah About Diet
Three Men In A Tub Hauled In For Questioning
Jack Didn't Make It Over the Candlestick
NASA Alert: Cow Jumped Over the Moon
Bobby Shafto Assumed Lost: 2 Weeks Sea Search
Hansel and Gretel Arrested for Crumb Littering

*

With Covid-19, masks are the new ID for people we see:
are they designer, homemade, store, or freebies available?
Judgment calls are quick, universal, you'll readily agree
in vogue since cave man days—perfected, generational.

Entanglement

happens when pairs or groups of particles are not independent
even when far away from one another: "spooky action at a
 distance"
as Albert Einstein described. Particles to have this interdependent
action happens when pairs or groups of particles are not
 independent.
But even if bizarre, those in quantum mechanics have defendants
backed with tests proving to unbelievers that this strange existence
action happens when pairs or groups of particles are not
 independent
even when far away from one another: "spooky action at a
 distance."

Clocks

Sundials are among the first clocks and wonder what changes technology will bring. There're museums and libraries dedicated to time keeping as well as organizations and associations like the National Watch and Clock Museum in Pennsylvania.

The first clock I remember is my grandfather's and then round black school ones. Each clock exudes a tale through its face, tick, hands, numbers, size, shape, color, and how old it is.

My alarm has graduated to an extra loud with shaker, red flashing face with battery backup which contrasts with my grandfather of mellow wood, engraved brass, pendulum, chimes. In between the boom and grandfather is a battery clock with distinctive black Baskerville numbers.

There Comes Such Days

There comes such days we turn back time
By a childhood nursery rhyme
Said in the midst of winter's night
Then fear the very rhyme outright
And turn distrustful of daytime.

Maybe all turns a pantomime
And tomorrow not worth the climb:
A "told by an idiot…" tale—
There comes such days.

How does sleep come in the meantime
Living under such pale moons? I'm
Sure many nights might have starlight
When midsummer dreams flood outright
After demure days of springtime—
There comes such days.

Black and White to Color

Many caught The Andy Griffith Show when it began airing on television in 1960: the characters turning into neighbors and Mayberry becoming ours—the barber shop, sidewalks, Andy's home, young Ronny Howard—American as apple pie in black and white.

Cauliflower sold for 10 cents each, Black-Eyed Peas were 10 cents a pound; Butch, Flat Top haircuts were both $2.00; the American flag in the sheriff's office and the school. The slow pace, caring, humor, comedy, was balm.

When it turned to color in Season 6, Andy's hair was lighter than I'd thought; Bee's best friend, Clara's hair should've been black like I'd imagined, while a strawberry blond Opie a big surprise. Floyd's mustache was the salt and pepper I'd imagined—the smudges on the school black board had many more shades of gray.

A Remodeling

The fast food place gave a sense of floating: gray floor, walls
repeating, table tops dazzling new by floor to ceiling pristine panes
of glass; I searched for anything familiar—but nothing offered a
  greeting.

My blue booth with tree-corner tare gone, I needed another seating
but in passing they all seems uninviting—to sit was a trespass:
the fast food place gave a sense of floating: gray floor, walls,
  repeating.

The trays seemed heavier, food cooled faster, ice cubes fleeting
so stared at them hoping it would become mine like in the past;
I searched for anything familiar—but nothing offered a greeting.

The walls were bare of even a clock so watched children
  competing
for fries across the way until their parents began to harass—
the fast food place gave a sense of floating: gray floor, walls
  repeating.

The trays were the same and sat straight as if waiting for a meeting
then oddly recalled last night's documentary about atomic mass: I
searched for anything familiar—but nothing offered a greeting.

Next time would be easier and it would be more enjoyable eating:
monotone colors were in vogue and were supposed to give class.
The fast food place gave a sense of floating: gray floor, walls
repeating: I searched for anything familiar—but nothing offered
  a greeting.

Geography

When I'd given up finding clues,
I gave away the mat of compressed
mosses, liverworts, and fossils,
uncovered burying leaves.

Yet, not ready to accept life
was a ball of twine without a
beginning, or Caroline's:
"Don't look to this world or
in yourself," I got out my
childhood atlas.

I was reassured that Wisconsin
was surrounded by Lake Superior
on the north, Lake Michigan on
the east, Minnesota on the west,
and the south by Illinois.

Each had a different pastel
shade so it must be true—
besides, the lakes had not moved.

Holding On

A familiar Yeats line is: "Things fall apart; the centre cannot hold"
is one we may recall trying to comprehend space, grasp the view
and our Milky Way is one among billions of an expanding fold.

It was Copernicus, Galileo, and Kepler, who studied the sky, told
us the Earth wasn't the center of everything—which much is due:
a familiar Yeats line is: "Things fall apart; the centre cannot hold."

It is disconcerting not to think the Sun a Greek God warming cold
Earth everyday with his gold chariot and fiery horses that flew—
and our Milky Way is one among billions of an expanding fold.

The popular myth of Daedalus and Icarus, father and son, sold
many with a moral: but instead of wax what if they'd used glue?
A familiar Yeats line is: "Things fall apart; the centre cannot hold."

Yeats wrote the line after World War I when events broke the mold;
not many years after, Hubble made the mind-bending breakthrough
and our Milky Way is one among billions of an expanding fold.

Scientific progress increases, challenges our human status, role—
the first picture taken of a Black Hole in now for your review;
a familiar Yeats line is: "Things fall apart; the centre cannot hold"
and our Milky Way is one among billions of an expanding fold.

Epilogue

Fog Hints

a 4th dimension with an ephemeral
catch-me-if-you-can of *Midsummer's
Night Dream*. When it rises is it
because air's warmer than earth—
or vice versa?

Patches of uneven size and thickness
pass quickly leaving you wondering
if it ever was; walking through it the
fear of falling off the Earth
sailing with Columbus.

About the Author

Carol Smallwood, MLS, MA, Marquis Lifetime Achievement Award recipient, is a literary judge, editor, and interviewer. Her 13th collection is *Thread, Forms, and Other Enclosures* (Main Street Rag Publishing Company, 2020). The Michigan resident's over five dozen edited books include *Women on Poetry: Writing, Revising, Publishing and Teaching,* on *Poets & Writers Magazine* list of Best Books for Writers.